YOUR KNOWLEDGE HAS VALUE

- We will publish your bachelor's and
  master's thesis, essays and papers

- Your own eBook and book -
  sold worldwide in all relevant shops

- Earn money with each sale

Upload your text at www.GRIN.com
and publish for free

Bibliographic information published by the German National Library:

The German National Library lists this publication in the National Bibliography; detailed bibliographic data are available on the Internet at http://dnb.dnb.de .

This book is copyright material and must not be copied, reproduced, transferred, distributed, leased, licensed or publicly performed or used in any way except as specifically permitted in writing by the publishers, as allowed under the terms and conditions under which it was purchased or as strictly permitted by applicable copyright law. Any unauthorized distribution or use of this text may be a direct infringement of the author s and publisher s rights and those responsible may be liable in law accordingly.

Imprint:

Copyright © 2016 GRIN Verlag, Open Publishing GmbH
Print and binding: Books on Demand GmbH, Norderstedt Germany
ISBN: 9783668359734

This book at GRIN:

http://www.grin.com/en/e-book/346597/the-fetishization-of-female-trauma-how-mozart-constructs-sovereignty-through

Lena Dassonville

The Fetishization of Female Trauma. How Mozart Constructs Sovereignty Through Maleness and Denies Sovereignty Through Femaleness

GRIN Publishing

GRIN - Your knowledge has value

Since its foundation in 1998, GRIN has specialized in publishing academic texts by students, college teachers and other academics as e-book and printed book. The website www.grin.com is an ideal platform for presenting term papers, final papers, scientific essays, dissertations and specialist books.

Visit us on the internet:

http://www.grin.com/

http://www.facebook.com/grincom

http://www.twitter.com/grin_com

The Fetishization of Female Trauma: How Mozart Constructs Sovereignty Through Maleness and Denies Sovereignty Through Femaleness

Written and composed by Lorenzo Da Ponte and Wolfgang Amadeus Mozart, *Don Giovanni* is the story of an Italian nobleman named Don Giovanni whose conquests are women and whose morals are questionable at best. Don Giovanni is a serial seducer, rapist, murderer, and infamous libertine. The opera follows Don Giovanni from the attempted rape of noblewoman Donna Anna to his ultimate damnation to hell. Aside from the alarming exposition and denouement, there is plenty disconcerting fodder within the main story arc of *Don Giovanni* as well. I aim to illuminate the sexual, familial, and the political power structures in *Don Giovanni* through the use of Lauren Berlant's theory of the intimate public sphere and Rousseau's theory of the body politic. More specifically, I wish to examine how through maleness, sovereignty is constructed and through femaleness, sovereignty is denied. Going beyond the contents of the libretto, I also endeavor to explore how Mozart fetishizes and desires female trauma through the music in *Don Giovanni*.

Some of the more interesting and revealing scenes in *Don Giovanni* are the interactions between men and women. In the very first scene, which shall be referred to later on as scene one, Don Giovanni is shown sneaking into the home of the Italian noblewoman Donna Anna while his servant, Leporello, waits outside. Don Giovanni attempts to rape Donna Anna while she protests, crying out "Idiot! You scream in vain. Who I am you'll never know!" (I.i.) To which Donna Anna replies in fear, "Help! Everyone! The betrayer… Scoundrel… Help! Everyone!" (I.i.) In response, Donna Anna's father, the Commendatore, arrives to defend his daughter's honor. "Leave her alone, wretch, and defend yourself," the Commendatore exclaims. "Thus you think to escape me... Fight!" (I.i) As Don Giovanni and the Commendatore begin to exchange blows, the Commendatore is mortally wounded and falls dead shortly after uttering his last words: "Help, assistance, all is ended! Oh, to die alone unfriended, vile assassin, thou'st undone me, heaven protect and guard my child!" (I.i) To summarize, Don Giovanni begins by trying to rape Donna Anna. He is unsuccessful because he is interrupted by her father, the Commendatore, who he later kills in a battle waged by the Commendatore to defend his daughter's honor. In this way, Donna Anna becomes something to be defended when breached. As the female, Donna Anna's honor (virginity) must be protected from a (male) power by her (male) father. Another vital scene, which will later be referred to as scene two, is the interaction between Masetto and Zerlina after Don Giovanni attempts to seduce Zerlina on her wedding night. Masetto angrily reject's Zerlina's attempts to make amends for being seduced by Don Giovanni. However, Zerlina apologizes successfully by fully submitting her body to Masetto. Zerlina states:

> But if I am not to blame? If I have been tricked by him? And then, what do you fear? Calm yourself, my love; he did not touch even the tips of my fingers. You don't believe it? Ungrateful one! Come here! Vent your anger! Kill me! Do everything you want to me, but afterwards, my Masetto, let us make peace. Beat me, beat me, my Masetto, beat your poor Zerlina. I'll stay here like a lamb and await your every blow... I'll let you pull my hair out, I'll let you gouge my eyes out, and then happily I will kiss your wonderfully sweet hands... Let's make up, my own true love" (I.iii)

Here, Zerlina completely submits herself to Masetto; offering herself up, she even condones her own murder. Masetto has complete power over Zerlina and she is subject to any punishment he deems fit. The entirety of the opera contains typical patriarchal familial structures in which women are subordinate to the men. No matter which family you look at in *Don Giovanni*, the males are dominant, and the females submissive.

It is here I wish to connect the patriarchal family structures in *Don Giovanni* to Berlant's theory of the intimate public sphere and Rousseau's theory of the body politic. Lauren Berlant's *The Queen of America Goes to Washington City: Essays on Sex and Citizenship* asks a deceptively complex question: what exactly is the nation? From this question, many more disseminate. (What constitutes the nation, how do we experience it? How do we understand our citizenship on an intimate level?) Instead of constructing the nation as a sovereign power to which we assign our loyalty, Berlant articulates the nation, and citizenship to the state, as a sort of lived experience, resounding intimately and sexually. For Berlant, citizenship has become inextricably interwoven with intimate and sexual interactions with the state. The public sphere, emblematic of a rational political polis and empirical discourse, is more a location of intimacy. According to Berlant, "The intimate public sphere of the present tense renders citizenship as a condition of social membership produced by personal acts and values, especially acts originating in or directed toward the family sphere" (Berlant 5). Thus, the public is not the source of civic engagement, but rather the projection of familial constructs of such citizenship. The intimate public sphere is fueled by an idealistic imaginary of the family as the root for identity and effectuation of what is construed as the state and its sovereign authority. This imaginary of the family "usurps the modernist promise of the culturally vital, multiethnic city" (Berlant 5). Thus, the imaginary of the family propagates traditional notions of community and familial structure. This allows the intimate public sphere to reproduce itself in a way that condenses the public into the private, sex into citizenship, home into state. Public discourse essentially becomes reflective of the private; to the point at which there seems to be no differentiation. The home is as much an extension of the state as citizenship is a form of sexual interaction with the sovereign power. With Berlant theorizing how the state operates, I turn to Rousseau to theorize the construction of the state itself. To Rousseau, it is inevitable at some point that a people will require a sort of governance in order to preserve their freedoms (Rousseau 87). By entering into civil society, our physical liberties are limited, but our civil liberties which motivate reason and morality are augmented (Rousseau 89). The community that is then formed is a "moral and collective body" (Rousseau 88). Elaborating on the structure of this community, Rousseau states:

> This public person so formed by the union of all other persons, formerly took the name of city, and now takes that of Republic or body politic; it is called by its members State when passive, Sovereign when active, and Power when compared with others like itself. Those who are associated in it take collectively the name of people, and severally are called citizens, as sharing in the sovereign power, and subjects, as being under the laws of the State" (Rousseau 88).

Thus, the sovereign is an entity comprised of members of the community— not just a single member as is commonly understood. The state takes on the power of those comprising it— the state and the people are one. While the sovereign is still subject to the social contract, the citizens are further confined. Not only are the citizens tied to the sovereign, they are also tied to the other individuals within the state. In that sense, the sovereign establishes primacy over its citizens. And, the state, though comprised of subjects, transcends citizenship. However, the citizen and the state are still collapsible to the extent that they are one. Like Berlant, Rousseau conflates the citizen and the state in albeit a less dystopian manner. However, there is a power derived from statehood which constructs the sovereign. The sovereign then may wield the power of statehood to which its members consented. But this state, which is more a scene of intimacy and sexual interaction than an space of political and rational dialogue, reproduces hegemonic discourse and power structures by subjugating its citizens. The citizen becomes subservient to the sovereign in that they are trapped within the intimate public sphere to exist within the confines of hegemonic structures and to obey the sovereign power.

In *Don Giovanni*, characters exist within a Rousseauean civil society. However, not all members of this society are created equal. The intimate relations within the opera, the couplings of Zerlina with Masetto and Donna Anna with the Commendatore and in strife with Don Giovanni, create a power struggle reminiscent of the struggle between citizen and state. The interaction in scene one encapsulates the intimate public sphere producing male dominance. When Don Giovanni attempts to rape Donna Anna, she is rescued by her father. To Don Giovanni, Donna Anna is something to be procured and utilized and to the Commendatore she is something to be guarded and defended. (Recall his last words: "…heaven protect and guard my child!" [I.i]) Not unlike a piece of property, Donna Anna is exchanged between males (From her father— to Don Giovanni [almost]— and to her husband, Don Ottavio.) Donna Anna's powerlessness is inextricable from the fact that she is a woman, a lacking womb, and a being with inherent sexuality. She is a subject of Don Giovanni's, Don Ottavio's, and the Commendatore's sovereignties. Donna Anna's citizenship is to her father, it is later transferred to Don Ottavio, and is nearly seized by Don Giovanni. Donna Anna is helplessly entangled within the intimate public sphere. For Donna Anna, citizenship and sexuality have been conflated so that through her sexuality, she becomes a citizen worthy of a state (recall the guarding of her virginity by her father and the coveting of her virginity by Don Giovanni.) The politics of the intimate public sphere then reproduce the patriarchal system of male dominance and female submission. Since the intimate public sphere condenses the state and the citizen into one, patriarchy becomes one with the state. Both males (Don Giovanni, the Commendatore, and Don Ottavio) and females (Donna Anna) comprise this body politic, but the ability to act as sovereign is reserved for the group which dominates. Thus, the singular man in *Don Giovanni* becomes the duality of citizen and sovereign— he is eligible for citizenship, and because of his maleness, sovereignty. Consequentially, the singular woman then must only inhabit the space of citizen as she is denied sovereignty of any kind.

Further, the construction of male sovereignty and female citizenship can also be identified in scene two with the interactions between Zerlina and Masetto. Zerlina gives her body over completely to Masetto. She relinquishes her autonomy and selfhood in order to appease her husband. In a sort of bizarre social contract, Zerlina gives up all of her physical liberties in order to gain the civil liberties of marriage with Masetto. By doing so, Masetto becomes a sovereign power. She is bound to him completely, and he to her only partially. She is his subject, while he is the state itself. The patriarchal political construct produced and propagated by the intimate public sphere allows for the construction of a male sovereignty and and female citizenship.

In *Queen of America*, Berlant establishes trauma as a desire of the state. According to Berlant, the act of possessing both citizenship and sovereignty (like the male characters in *Don Giovanni*) has become a deeply intimate sort of identity which produces a desire for trauma— for the privileged to experience the fetishized subjugation of the subjugated. Trauma is inaccessible for the sovereign, so he seeks to construct it in a sort of Lacanian Imaginary. Though the Imaginary's demand is unsatisfiable and ultimately an illusion, this does not stop the state from fetishizing and desiring the elusive trauma of the female. Mozart, as the ultimate sovereign, constructor of both states and world, seeks to experience or at least spectate female trauma. He does this in two ways: by de-vulgarizing rape, effectively constructing sexual assault as a facet of entertainment and making the suffering of women something to be observed and surveilled. The act of depicting rape in front of an audience is questionable in and of itself. To make sexual assault something that is observed by onlookers is to place the audience in a strange space of viewing pleasure. The audience watches *Don Giovanni* for entertainment, thus the various sexual assaults portrayed in the opera (not to mention one rape scene occurs at a party) become a part of the audience's viewing pleasure. This is not to say that sexual assault should not be depicted, but rather the manner in which it is done is key. Mozart frames the first attempted rape scene, Don Giovanni's attack on Donna Anna, with comedy. When Don Giovanni murders the Commendatore and calls out to Leporello asking where he is, Leporello replies, "Who's dead, th'old man, or you Sir?" (I.i) This moment of comic relief detracts from the heinous crimes just committed. Rape and murder is followed with jest. Mozart also composes exciting, riveting scores for Don Giovanni, and mundane, unimaginative music for everyone else. Immediately, the audience is drawn to the charismatic musicality surrounding Don Giovanni. By surrounding the act of rape with comedy and the rapist with captivating music, Mozart de-vulgarizes rape, effectively constructing sexual assault as a facet of entertainment. The depravity and obscenity of rape is downplayed by Mozart's insistence on romanticizing the rapist and downplaying the severity and ramifications of sexual assault. Ultimately, Mozart seeks to observe the suffering of women. By depicting and meticulously manipulating the emotional distress and suffering of

Donna Elvira, Donna Anna, and Zerlina, Mozart fetishizes their trauma and strives to make it his own. The music of Mozart's women tends to be either hysterically sorrowful or angrily zealous —either a perpetual melancholy or a defiant misery. Their lamentations are a product of their traumas, something which Mozart eerily desires to construct. Through observation, Mozart as a sovereign desires the depiction of female trauma. He can not comprehend it, so he must make it hiss subject to be observed and surveilled— for him, the feminine is the subject of both desire and derision.

By looking at the gender politics and the entrapment of characters within the intimate public sphere, Mozart's *Don Giovanni* constructs sovereignty through maleness and denies sovereignty through femaleness. And, Mozart himself, as the ultimate sovereign power, plays into the state's fetishization and desire of trauma by de-vulgarizing rape and making the suffering of female characters a sort of spectator event.

Works Cited

Berlant, Lauren Gail. *The Queen of America Goes to Washington City: Essays on Sex and Citizenship*. Durham, NC: Duke UP, 1997. Print.

Mozart, Wolfgang Amadeus, and Lorenzo Da Ponte. "*Don Giovanni*." Opera Guide: The Virtual Opera House, n.d. Web. 13 Apr. 2016.

Rousseau, Jean Jacques. "*The Social Contract*." *Core Text Reader*. 2016. 81-104. Print.

YOUR KNOWLEDGE HAS VALUE

- We will publish your bachelor's and master's thesis, essays and papers

- Your own eBook and book - sold worldwide in all relevant shops

- Earn money with each sale

Upload your text at www.GRIN.com
and publish for free